Méthode d'anglais pour l'école primaire

Domino & Co.

Cycle 3
Niveau 1

Corinne Marchois
Caroline Forshaw

Me

Name ....

Class ....

Teacher ....

School ....

Didier
13, rue de l'Odéon, 75006 Paris

Table of contents / Sommaire

Once upon a time, Alice was reading a story when a white rabbit ran past. Sir Henry was late. He was looking at his watch. He was running very fast and ... oops!

1 Hello! What's your name?

A Hello!

B What's your name?

Date:

1 Ask and write!

Domino	Shakespeare

2 Glue your picture!

My name's

....

I remember!

C A song!

Hello, hello, hello,
My name's Domino,
I'm Domino.
And you, what's your name?
Are you John, or are you Jessy?
Are you Mike, or are you Eve?

D What's his/her name?

E Sounds

Date:

3 Glue the picture!

MY FAVOURITE STAR

His/Her name's ....

4 Complete the sentences!

..... name's William Shakespeare.

..... name's Marilyn Monroe.

...... name's Gandhi.

5 Listen and colour! [h]

1 2 3 4 5 6 7 8

2 What colour is it?

A I mix and mix and mix...

B What colour is it?

1 Colour and complete!

It's ....

It's ....

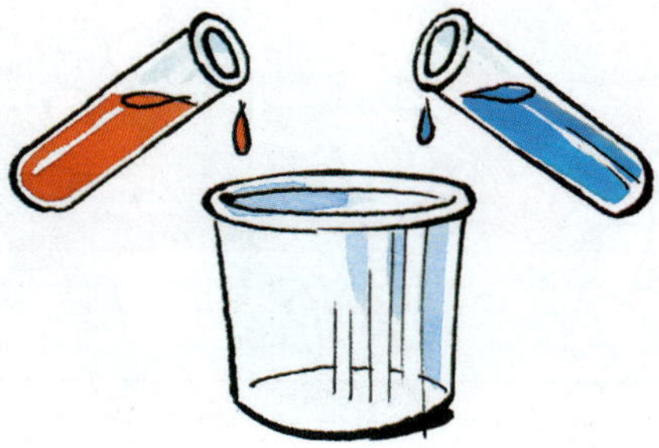

It's ....

My scientific experiments

Yellow and red make orange.

Blue and .... make green.

.... and .... make purple.

2 Listen and join! [r]

C Is it red?

D A shapes game

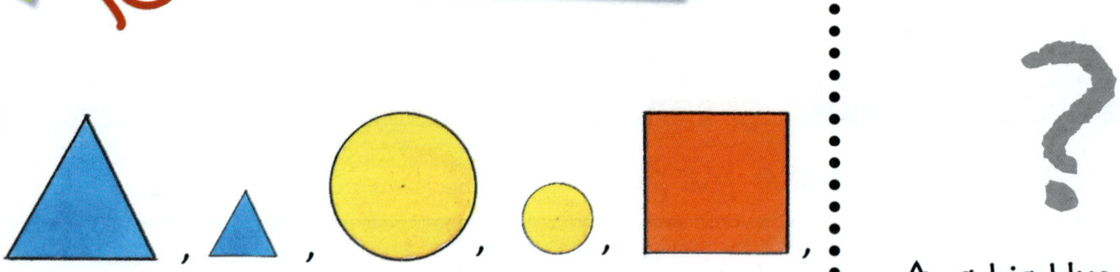

A. a big blue square
B. a small red square
C. a small yellow triangle

E What is your favourite colour?

Date:

3 Read and answer!

4 Draw and dictate!

Pupil A

........, ..., ..., ...

Pupil B

........, ..., ..., ...

5 Draw and complete!

My favourite colour is ....

I remember!

3 Guy Fawkes' night!

A A counting rhyme

B Colourful numbers

C Additions and subtractions

Date:

1 Complete!

..........., ... How are you?
..........., ... Open the door!
..........., ... My watch ticks.
..........., ... Don't be late!
..........., ... Can I borrow your pen?
..........., ... Stretch yourselves!

2 Listen and write!

3 Listen and circle! [θ]

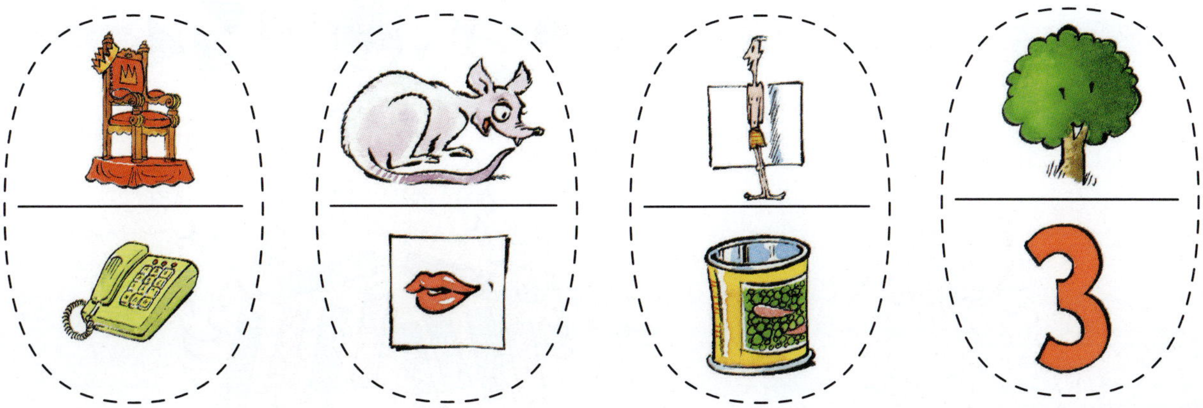

D Bonfire

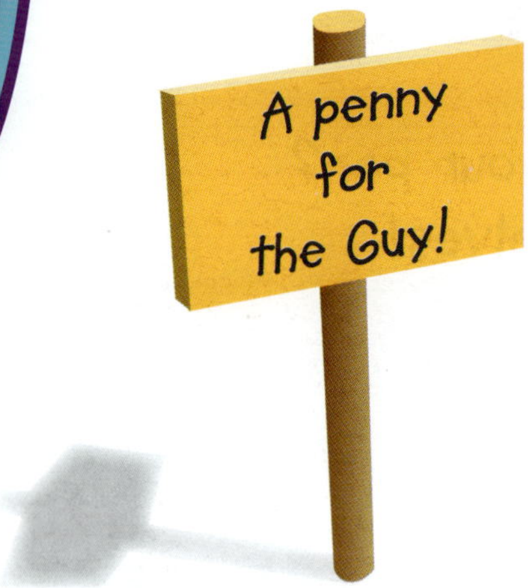

E Guy Fawkes' rhyme

Remember, remember
The 5th of November.
Gunpowder, treason and plot...

F How many stars are there?

Date: ....

4 Listen and complete!

My guy is ....

My guy is ....

My guy is ....

My guy is ....

5 Draw your guy and complete!

This is my guy.

He is ....

....

....

6 Complete!

There are .... stars.

There are .... triangles.

There is .... guy.

I remember!

4 All about me!

A How old are you?

Come to my birthday party
To: Domino
From: Jack
When: 3.00 pm.
Where: 92, Smith Street Bolton
RSVP: 0861 312465

B Happy Birthday!

Date:

1 Read and write!

....

And you? ....

2 Listen and join!

How old is Daniel? ....

C Hello!

D Oh dear!

Date:

3 Read and replace the vowels!

And you?

My ....

....

4 Look, choose and speak!

Kate | Jack | Emily | Lucy | Matthew

London | Aberdeen | Liverpool | Northampton | Paris

London	Aberdeen	Liverpool	Northampton	Paris
1) oO	1) ooO	1) Ooo	1) Ooo	1) Oo
2) Oo	2) Ooo	2) oOo	2) oOo	2) oO

5 Read and colour!

- Where do you live?
- Where does Kate live?
- Where does Jack live?

- She lives in ....
- He lives in ....
- I live in ....

I remember!

5 I know it!

1 Je reconnais les sons

Entends-tu [r] ?

Mot 1 : oui non
Mot 2 : oui non
Mot 3 : oui non

Entends-tu [h] ?

Mot 1 : oui non
Mot 2 : oui non
Mot 3 : oui non

Entends-tu [θ] ?

Mot 1 : oui non
Mot 2 : oui non
Mot 3 : oui non

2 J'écoute et je complète

Name
Age 10
Address 5 Sheraton Street
London W12 88H
Phone number (0)20 8707 4255

Name
Age 9
Address 11, Finch Lane
Hampton W38 EU
Phone number 019 0276 5285

Name
Age 8
Address 38 Fitzwarren Street
Salford M6 5JF
Phone number 0113 264 72 38

Name
Age 10
Address 32 Clayton Gardens
Liverpool SW5 7HR
Phone number 0151 452 9432

Name
Age 9
Address 92 Royal Road
London W10 5GB
Phone number 020 7832 2453

Date:

3 Je lis et j'associe

◯ Good night!

◯ Good morning!

◯ Good afternoon!

◯ Goodbye!

◯ Good evening!

4 Je lis, je dessine et je colorie

Draw a small blue triangle. Draw a big red circle and a small yellow square.

5 Je lis et je sélectionne

1

He is happy.
He is sad.

2

He is fat.
She is fat.

3

He is tall and fat.
He is tall and thin.
He is small and thin.

6 J'écris les mots au bon endroit

name	Her	is	Helen	.

blue	the	?	Is	triangle

.	square	red	is	big	It	a

Quiz

1 - Guy Fawkes a vécu vers :	A) 1400	B) 1600	C) 1800
2 - Guy Fawkes était :	U) protestant	O) catholique	S) anglican
3 - Guy Fawkes a voulu tuer :	N) le roi James 1er H) le prince Charles		G) la reine Elisabeth
4 - Il s'est révolté :	J) contre les impôts de plus en plus lourds F) pour stopper les lois anti catholiques		K) mettre fin à l'esclavage
5 - Le complot a eu lieu :	I) le 5 novembre 1605 M) le 5 novembre 1805		L) le 5 décembre 1605

Date:

7 Je parle

6 - Il a voulu mettre feu au parlement avec 36 barils de poudre : R) vrai T) faux

7 - On célèbre ce complot chaque année en Angleterre en faisant brûler un personnage de paille et en faisant des feux d'artifice : E) vrai V) faux

Réponds et dessine :

6 Let's go to school!

A Hi, how are you?

B How are they?

Date:

1 Listen and draw!

A B C D

2 Read and number!

◯ I'm fine.
◯ I'm not very well.
◯ I'm so-so.
◯ I'm OK.

3 Read and circle the right answer!

	True	False
Domino is scared.	H	S
Helen is sad.	I	A
Eddy is sick.	C	P
Sir Henry is tired.	P	K
The postman is furious.	Y	O

Hooray! I am _ _ _ _ _ _!

C In class

D In my room

Date: ....

4 Look and colour!

.... here .... up .... down

5 Read and write!

....	
1 pencil case	£2.99
scissors	£1.99
1 glue	39p

....	
1 ruler	20p
1 exercise book	£1.99
1 schoolbag	£21.00

....	
1 rubber	15p
1 pen	£3.99
1 pencil	7p

6 Read and answer!

I remember!

7 It's Christmas!

A The winner!

Lotto *Play and win!* **Lotto extra**

1	2	3	4	~~5~~	~~6~~	7	8	9	10	~~11~~	12
13	14	15	16	17	~~18~~	19	20	21	22	23	24
25	26	~~27~~	28	29	30	31	32	33	~~34~~	35	36
37	38	39	40	~~41~~	42	43	44	45	46	47	48
49	Lucky Dip				Choose 7 numbers						

~~1~~	~~2~~	3	4	5	6	~~7~~	8	9	10	11	12
~~13~~	14	~~15~~	16	17	18	19	20	21	22	~~23~~	24
25	26	27	28	29	30	31	32	33	34	35	36
37	38	~~39~~	40	41	42	43	44	45	46	47	48
49	Lucky Dip				Choose 7 numbers						

B We wish you a merry Xmas!

Date:

1 Listen and write!

2 Read and write!

3 Listen and join! [aɪ]

C Christmas morning

D Domino writes an important Xmas letter

Dear Father Christmas,

My name is Domino.
I am a good little robot.
Please, I'd like a kite and a bike.

Love from
Domino
XXX

P.S. I'd like a computer, too, PLEASE!!!

Date:

4 Listen and write!

5 Look carefully and write!

It's ....   It's ....   It's ....

I remember!

8 Sunny days!

A What's the date today?

Teacher: Mrs. Brown					
Class: Year 6	Monday	Tuesday	Wednesday	Thursday	Friday
8.55	Registration	Registration	Registration	Registration	Registration
9.10	Assembly	Assembly	Assembly	Assembly	Assembly
9.30 - 10.20	Literacy	Numeracy	Literacy	Numeracy	Literacy
10.20 - 10.35			Break		

B The year

January 15 th 2006

February March April May

June July August September

October November December

nd rd st

Date:

1 Read and complete!

M......................., T......................., W.......................

We play, play, play!

T......................., F......................., S.......................

It's a happy day!

And S.......................?

We're on holiday!

2 Write the date!

Today is ....

Yesterday was

....

Tomorrow will be

....

3 Cross the odd man out! [eɪ]

A   

....

B   

....

C   

C What's the weather like?

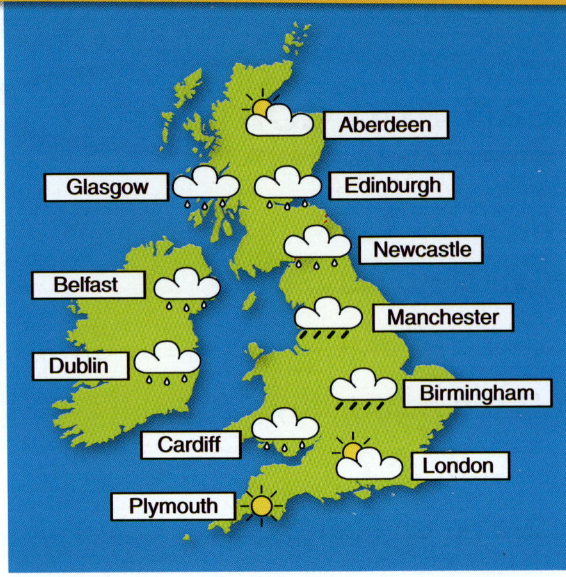

D My holidays

London

Leeds

Manchester

Dublin

Date:

4 Listen and join!

Liverpool Oxford Cambridge Brighton

5 Read and complete!

I remember!

9 Families

A The British Royal Family

Date:

1 Draw, write and speak!

My (ideal) family

2 Read and write!

have | got | I | sisters | two | .

....

brother | ? | you | Have | got | a

....

haven't | got | brother | a | . | I

....

B A song!

I'm Domino!
My brother's called Bingo,
My sister's called Mango!
My father's name is Tomato
My mother's name is Potato!
My grandfather is Buffalo,
My grandmother is Rainbow!
We've got two cats,
We call them Rolo and Polo!

C The alphabet

Date:

3 Listen, colour and write!

A B C D E F G H I J K

L M N O P Q R S T U

V W X Y Z

_ _ _ _ _ _ _ _ is easy and fun!

4 Read and write!

a	☆	k	+	u	↘
b	◎	l	ᔕ	v	---
c	□	m	ℓ	w	≡
d	△	n	ɣ	x	⋈
e	@	o	∞	y	♡
f	☾	p	∇	z	◈
g	⌓	q	⎍		
h	▽	r	◁		
i	▭	s	ɷ		
j	••	t	┌		

....

....

....

I remember!

10 Animals

A They love pets!

We're beautiful

Emma and Toby

My holiday with Granny and Patch

Hello Goldie

I love my hamster

Date:

1 Read and write their names!

Hello Henry!

Thank you! I've got 5 animals:
The black cat is called Polo.
The grey cat is Rolo.
The fat mouse is Bo and the thin mouse is called Lo.
And of course, the big brown dog (tired...) is Choco.

Love,

Domino

2 Describe your animal!

photo

3 Listen and tick the column!

Singular								
Plural								

B A song!

If you're happy and you know it:

clap your hands!
stamp your feet!
turn your body!
shake your head!
move your legs
wave your arms!

C Find Helen

Date:

4 Describe Helen!

Helen has got long, ... hair.

She is 9 .... old, and she is tall.

She's got .... eyes and a little ....

Her jeans are .... and she's got

a long .... pullover.

She's nice!

5 Fill in the form!

My best friend

Name:

Address:

Age:

Description:

I remember!

11 I know it!

1 Je reconnais les sons

[ɪ] pink
[iː] green
[aɪ] five
[eɪ] eight

2 J'écoute et je relie

Date:

3 J'écoute et j'entoure

A

B

C

4 Je lis et je dessine

He's got a little body and a big green head. He's got one short arm and seven legs. He's got long blue hair and three eyes: one eye is red and two are pink. He's got a mouth with two long teeth.

I AM SCARED!!!!

5 Je lis et je sélectionne

My name / time / game is Caroline.
I'm eleven dear / years / bikes old.
I sit / live / have in Manchester.
I have got / go / guy brown hair.
My brother is / are / am called Johnny.

6 J'écris

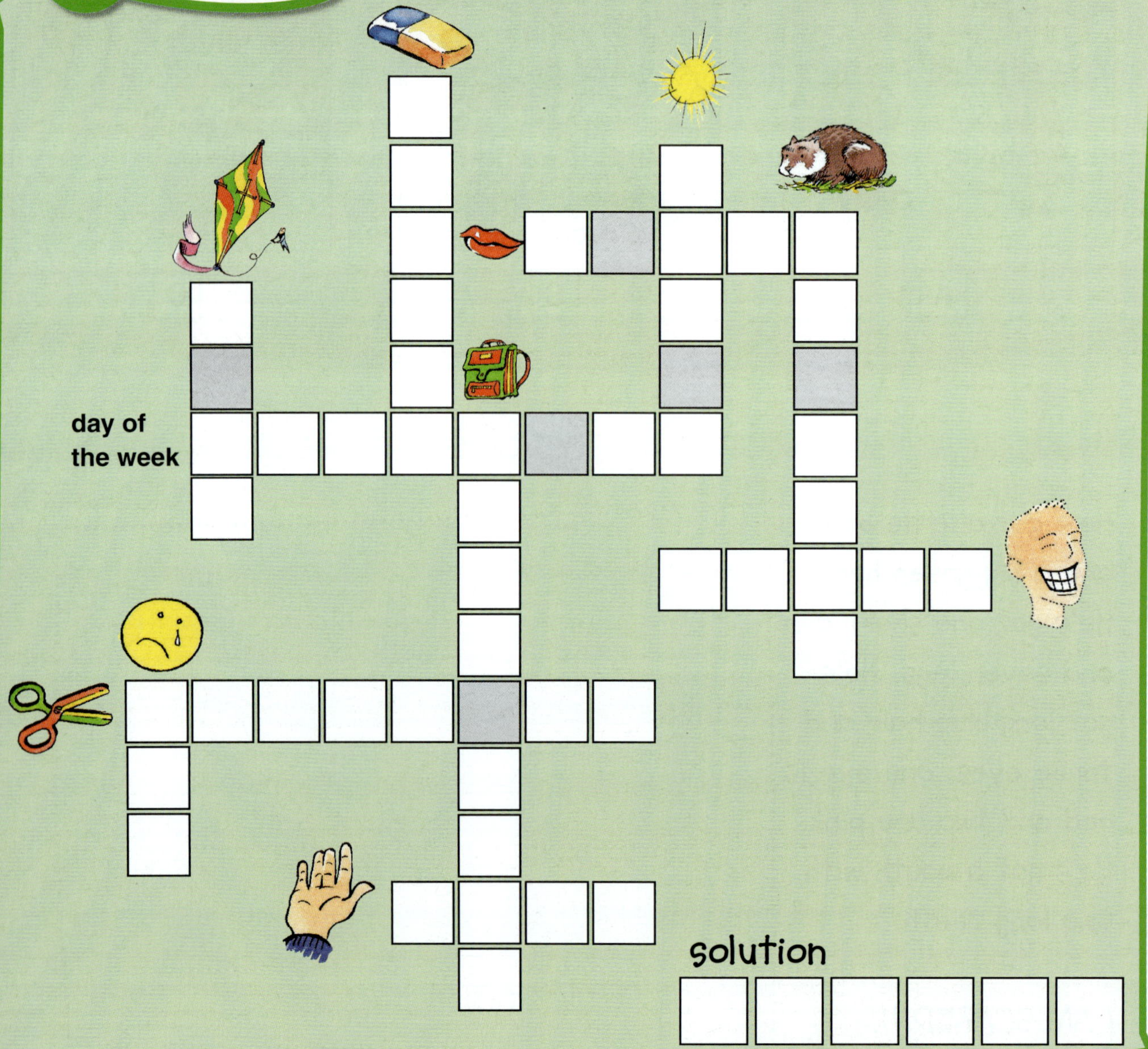

Date:

7 Je parle

Quiz

Vrai (✔) ou faux (✘) :

Le Père Noël s'appelle soit *Father Christmas* soit *Santa-Claus*.	
Le lendemain de Noël, appelé *Boxing Day*, est férié en Angleterre.	
Les enfants reçoivent leurs cadeaux le 26 décembre.	
Le *Christmas pudding* est une entrée typique pour Noël.	
Les enfants placent leurs chaussons au pied du sapin le 24 au soir.	
Les cartes de vœux sont envoyées avant Noël.	
Dans un *cracker*, on trouve une blague, un chapeau en papier et un petit cadeau.	

12 Eating and drinking

A Breakfast time

B Food groups

1 Read and number!

2 Separate the words!

marmaladeeggbakedbeanstoastcoffeeteabaconjammilkcerealsorangejuicechocolatebreadbutterbreakfast.

•anegg•twoeggsoneeggthreeeggssixeggs•eleveneggs•eighteggsfiveeggs•

C St Patrick's Day

Date:

3 Listen and number! [tʃ] / [dʒ]

1 2

4 Ask and write!

Do you like... ?	Domino			
orange juice	Yes, I do.			
coffee	No, I don't.			
tea	No, I don't.			
cereals	Yes, I do.			
bread	Yes, I do.			
marmalade	Yes, I do.			

I remember!

13 Where are the Easter eggs?

A Happy Easter!

Date:

1 Read and complete!

At [redacted], the [redacted] brings chocolate [redacted]. People write [redacted]. It's traditional to eat [redacted].

2 Look and number!

Happy Birthday! 1

Thank you! 2

Good morning! 3

Goodbye! 4

Merry Christmas! 5

3 Listen and colour!

[ʌ] [ɜː]

[ʌ]

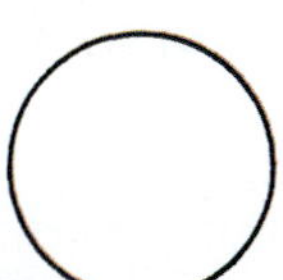

[ɜː]

B What's in the classroom?

C A song!

Is it under?
Is it next to?
Is it here?
Is it there?
O O O Where is it? (bis)
I don't know (bis)

Is it in front of?
Is it in front of?
Is it behind?
Is it between?
O O O Where is it? (bis)
I don't know (bis)

Are they under?
Are they next to?
Are they on?
Are they in?
O O O Where are they? (bis)
Here they are! (bis)

Date:

4 Look and write!

What's different?

....

....

....

....

....

....

....

5 Complete!

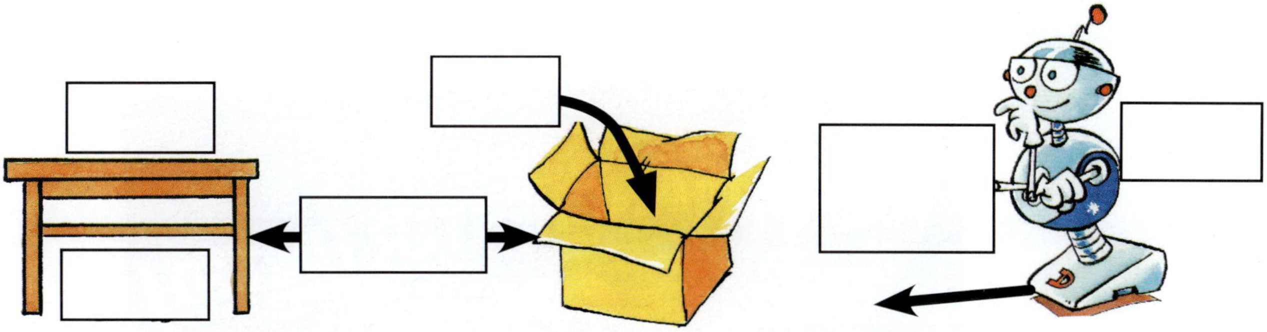

I remember!

14 Can you do it?

A Sports Day

Date:

1 Listen and colour!

Sir Henry: ◯
me: ◯

Sir Henry: ◯
me: ◯

Sir Henry: ◯
me: ◯

Sir Henry: ◯
me: ◯

Sir Henry: ◯
me: ◯

Sir Henry: ◯
me: ◯

Sir Henry: ◯
me: ◯

Sir Henry: ◯
me: ◯

Sir Henry: ◯
me: ◯

2 Look and complete!

Sir Henry can .... and ....,
but he can't .... and ....

I can ...., but I can't ....

B Ready, steady go!

Date:

3 Listen and join! [ɒ]/[ɔː]

[ɒ]

 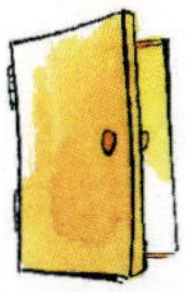    

[ɔː]

4 Who is the champion?

House name:								
Event: / Name:	100 metres race	4× 100m relay	3-legged race 50metres	Sack race 50 metres	Egg + spoon race 100 metres	Long jump	High jump	
Domino	30sec.		1 min 05s	1 min 55s	Abandon	1m.45cm	85cm	

I remember!

15 I know it!

1 J'écoute et j'entoure

Question N°1 : ↗ ↘

Question N°2 : ↗ ↘

Question N°3 : ↗ ↘

Question N°4 : ↗ ↘

Question N°5 : ↗ ↘

2 J'écoute et je choisis

3 J'écoute et je dessine

Date:

4 Je lis et j'associe

1

2

3

5

4

Imagine it is breakfast time and you are the breakfast for a giant with very big ears. Sophie is very scared of the giant but she discovers he is a friend, a big friendly giant.

He has got a lucky golden ticket in his Wonka's Whipple-Scrumptious Fudgemallow Delight. He visits a fabulous sweet factory and is very, very happy.

This eight-year old boy lives with his grandmother. She is very old and disagreeable. She's got a very long nose. He doesn't like his grandmother so he experiments and mixes up a specially invented drink.

She is only five years old but she can read and she can do maths. She has got lots of books.

Aunt Spiker is tall and thin and Aunt Sponge is short and fat and they are very cruel to their nephew. His life changes with magic, an enormous fruit and some big insect friends.

5 J'écris

Domino fait une enquête. Il interroge son ami Daniel. Voici sa réponse :
« Hello Domino, I can't swim but I can play cricket and I can ski.
I don't like baked beans and I don't like milk but I like Easter eggs.
Goodbye! »
Maintenant, reporte les informations concernant Daniel dans le tableau. Puis complète dans le tableau la colonne qui te concerne (me), et écris un petit texte pour parler de toi. Tu peux t'aider de celui de Daniel.

Can you ... ?	Daniel	me
swim		
play cricket		
ski		

Do you like ... ?	Daniel	me
baked beans		
milk		
Easter eggs		

....

....

....

Quiz

Colorie la case qui correspond à la bonne réponse.

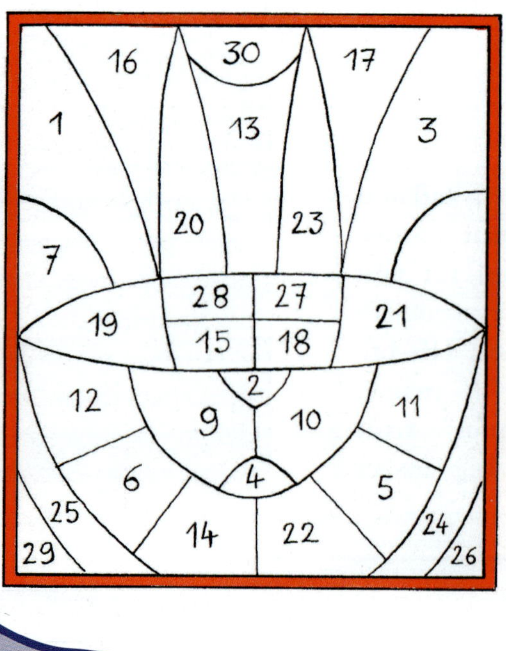

a. Pâques se dit
1) Ostern 2) Easter 3) Ice-cream.

b. Pour Pâques, les enfants
4) cherchent des œufs en chocolat dans le jardin
5) font une super omelette
6) passent en chantant de maison en maison pour obtenir de l'argent.

c. Des jeux sont organisés à l'occasion des fêtes de Pâques
7) un lancer d'œufs
8) une course avec un œuf en équilibre sur la tête
9) une course pendant laquelle il faut pousser un œuf en bas d'une colline.

d. À l'occasion des fêtes de Pâques, on mange un petit pain appelé
10) hot cross bun 11) hot dog 12) hot bread.

Date:

6 Je parle

e. Pour Pâques, les élèves ont
13) un week-end prolongé 14) une journée d'excursion au bord de la mer
15) deux semaines de vacances juste avant.

f. Souvent, pour les fêtes de Pâques, les écoles organisent
16) une kermesse 17) un bal 18) une « chasse » aux œufs.

g. St Patrick est fêté en 19) Angleterre 20) Irlande 21) Ecosse.

h. St Patrick est fêté le 22) 17 février 23) 17 mars 24) 17 avril.

i. La couleur symbolique de cette fête est le 25) rouge 26) bleu 27) vert.

j. La plante symbolique de cette fête est 28) le trèfle 29) le poireau 30) la rose.

Crédits photographiques

P.4 : © Butler Adam/Abaca - **P.6 :** (mg) © Walt Disney/Collection Cristophel ; (md) © Dan Chung/REUTERS - **P.10 :** Heather Weston/Botanica/Getty Images - **P.13 :** © Karin Rickmann/ www.fotocommunity.de - **P.14:** © Collections/ John Wender - **P.16 :** (hg) Getty Images/Taxi - **P.24 :** © Bob Krist/CORBIS - **P.26 :** © Corinne Marchois - **P.28 :** (bg) © Steve Lupton/CORBIS ; (bd) © Rick Barrentine/CORBIS - **P.30 :** © Mark M. Lawrence/CORBIS - **P. 34 :** (md) © Rupert Horrox/CORBIS ; (mg) © Annie Griffiths Belt/CORBIS ; (bg) © Michael Nicholson/CORBIS ; (bd)©Milepost 92 1/2 /CORBIS - **P.36 :** (left to right) © Tim Graham/CORBIS ; © Tim Graham/CORBIS ; © Tim Graham/CORBIS ; © Tim Graham/CORBIS ; © CORBIS ; ©Tim Graham/CORBIS ; © Tim Graham/CORBIS ; ©Tim Graham/CORBIS; © Tim Graham/CORBIS ; © CORBIS - **P.40 :** (hg) © Chris Jones/CORBIS, (hd) © Strauss/Curtis/CORBIS ; (c) © Ronnie Kaufman/CORBIS ; (bg) © Nancy Brown/CORBIS ; (bd) ©Laura Dwight/CORBIS - **P.42 :** (bg) John Smith/Circa Photo Library (bd) John Smith/Circa Photo Library - **P.48 :** (hc) ©David Ball/CORBIS - **P.50 :** (hc) Paul Faith/PA/EMPICS ; (mc) Michael Stephens/PA/EMPICS - **P.52 :** (hc) Westh Haydn West/PA/EMPICS ; (bg) Collections - **P.56 :** (hg) © Roy Peters/Report digital-Rea ;(mg) © Roy Peters/Report digital-Rea ; (md) © Roy Peters/Report digital-Rea ; (bc) Phil Noble/PA/EMPICS - **P.58 :** (hc) Adam Davey/EMPICS ; (mc) Adam Davey/EMPICS ; (bc) Adam Davey/EMPICS - **P.61 :** (hg) ; (hc) ; (hd) ; (mg) ; (md) : © Quentin Blake, reprinted with kind permission of AP Watt Ltd on behalf of Quentin Blake

Conception graphique couverture et intérieur, pictos : David Bart
Illustrations : Bruno Conquet
Mise en page : David Bart
Photogravure : Labogravure

Imprimé en France
Achevé d'imprimer en mai 2005 par l'Imprimerie CLERC - Dépôt légal : 5569/01